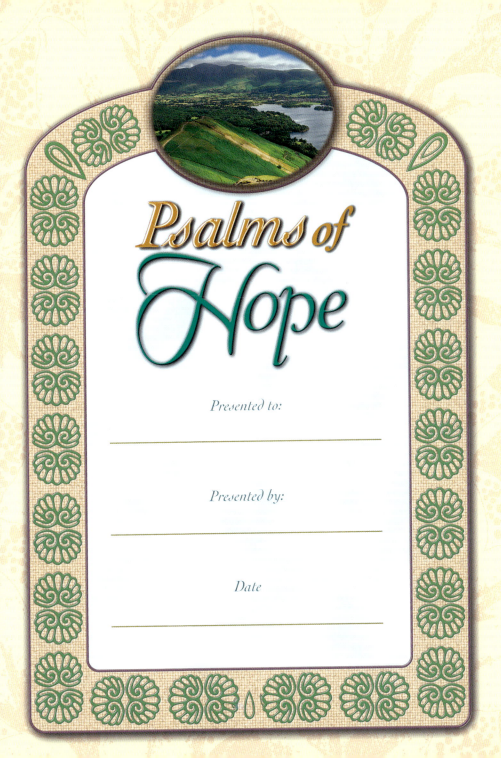

Psalms of *Hope*

Presented to:

_____

Presented by:

_____

Date

_____

Psalms of Hope

God's Gift of Comfort, Peace, and Encouragement

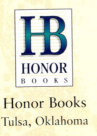

Honor Books

Tulsa, Oklahoma

Psalms of Hope
ISBN 1-56292-621-7
Copyright © 2002 by GRQ Ink, Inc.
1948 Green Hills Blvd.
Franklin, Tennessee 37067

Published by Honor Books
P.O. Box 55388
Tulsa, Oklahoma 74155

Developed by GRQ Ink, Inc.
Manuscript written and compiled by representatives of Snapdragon Editorial Group, Inc.
Cover and text design by Whisner Design Group
Composition by Educational Publishing Concepts, Inc.

Find rest, O my soul,
in God alone;
my hope comes from him.
He alone is my rock and my salvation;
he is my fortress,
I will not be shaken.

PSALMS 62:5-6 NIV

The Light of God's Love

*The L*ORD *is God,*
And he has made his light shine upon us.

PSALM 118:27 NIV

*O*ur problems always seem most daunting just before the dawn—right before the morning light climbs above the horizon and

slips quietly into the room. In that darkest hour, shadows of fear and discouragement often threaten to overwhelm us. But the morning light chases away the nighttime, restoring our perspective, filling us with hope, and offering us the promise of a bright new day!

The light of God's love is much like the morning sunlight. It dispels darkness from our hearts and sweeps away shadows of fear and discouragement. It renders harmless specters of condemnation that would harshly remind us of past failures. God's wondrous light allows us to see ourselves as He sees us—forgiven, new creatures, ready to begin again.

*L*ORD, I thank You for flooding my heart with the light of Your love and for illuminating the shadows and bringing a bright, shining morning of hope to my life.

THE LORD is my light and my salvation;
Whom shall I fear?
The LORD is the strength of my life;
Of whom shall I be afraid?

PSALM 27:1 NKJV

Mended Hearts

The LORD is close to the brokenhearted
and saves those who are crushed in spirit.

PSALM 34:18 NIV

Few people pass through life without feeling the sting of betrayal, the loss of friendship, or the failure of important relationships. At those times, we often feel that the pain of a broken heart will cling to us for the rest of our days and that we will never be whole again. Sometimes we even wonder if God still loves us.

God does love us, purely, simply, and unconditionally. Even if our pain is the result of our own actions, God's love does not condemn us. It urges us forward, calling us to forgive ourselves, make amends, and become better people. His love is constant and predictable. It is the one thing on which we can depend. And with the assurance of His love comes hope—hope that we will love again, trust again, offer our hearts again.

Father, thank You for the promise of Your constant love and the hope it brings to my life.

$\mathcal{M}$y flesh and my heart may fail,
but God is the strength of my heart
and my portion forever.

Psalm 73:26 niv

A Flame Rekindled

I wait for the LORD, *my soul waits,*
and in his word I hope.

PSALM 130:5 NRSV

A blazing wood fire is glorious, but when it's spent, nothing remains but white-gray ash—a somber contrast to the rough-cut log that once lay on the hearth and the colorful flames that danced high in the air, filling the room with warmth.

At times we may feel that our lives are reduced to ashes, that our strength is gone, and that the flame we once carried inside is cold and colorless. But God promises that even at our lowest point, even when we feel there is nothing left with which to rebuild our lives, He is there to rekindle the flame within us. His indwelling Spirit offers hope and strength to begin again, and His never-failing love shines brightly on our path, illuminating each step we take.

LORD GOD, I thank You that the fire of Your Spirit brings new life to my body and soul. I will place my life in Your hands and my hope in Your faithfulness and love.

*L*ead me by your truth and teach me,
for you are the God who saves me.
All day long I put my hope in you.

PSALM 25:5 NLT

Never Alone

I am continually with thee:
thou hast holden me by my right hand.
Thou shalt guide me with thy counsel,
and afterward receive me to glory.

PSALMS 73:23-24

A solitary tree standing in the middle of a field may appear to be deserted by all else. In fact, however, it is not. The warmth of the sun kisses that tree; the gentle breezes caress it; the fellowship of birds on the wing gladden it; and a small underground universe of lively creatures stimulate it.

We all experience loneliness at some time in our lives. Loneliness is natural and should be appreciated rather than feared. In seasons of loneliness, we discover that we are never *truly* alone—no more than that solitary tree. People we barely notice during times of social prosperity— neighbors, long-forgotten acquaintances, others who move quietly in and out of our daily lives—surround us and can become valuable friends. But the greatest discovery is that God is constantly with us, warming us with His love, and we can learn to hope in Him.

FATHER, during those times when I feel the ache of loneliness, help me to remember that You are never more than a whispered prayer away.

I love the LORD because he hears
and answers my prayers.
Because he bends down and listens,
I will pray as long as I have breath!

PSALMS 116:1-2 NLT

*G*od, we thank you;
we thank you because you are near.
We tell about the miracles you do.

PSALM 75:1 NCV

A Personal Passage

He reached down from on high and took hold of me;
he drew me out of deep waters.

PSALM 18:16 NIV

*E*ach life is a journey—a uniquely
personal passage through time. As we
travel through difficult places, we need
not give in to hopelessness. God is able to
bring us safely to our destination when we
place our trust in Him.

God is the Author of each journey. He knows the way through
every dark and frightening valley. He knows the safest path along
each high and treacherous mountain trail. God knows where the
cool, refreshing waters flow and where we can find the provisions to
meet each of our needs. He shares the weight of the burden we carry
and causes us to lie down and rest in lush green meadows. He gives
us hope and courage as we walk with Him, step by step, one day at a
time.

*L*ORD, as I face the challenges of my personal journey through life, I
am thankful for Your presence that guides and protects me.

*Y*ou will show me the way of life,
granting me the joy of your presence
and the pleasures of living with you forever.

PSALM 16:11 NLT

Plenty of Time

A thousand years mean nothing to you!
They are merely a day gone by
or a few hours in the night.

PSALM 90:4 CEV

*T*ime is both an enemy and a friend. We do our best to conquer it, and yet it continually slips through our fingers. We measure our lives, our successes, and our productivity in terms of minutes, hours, days, and weeks. We often lose our hope in the future and in the fulfillment of our dreams as time passes.

God isn't subject to *our* concept of time, for He is the Master of the universe. When we place our trust in Him, we can know with certainty that we have all the time we need to do what He has created us to do and that we have plenty of time to become all that He created us to be. When we present our dreams to God, we learn that our brightest hour is always ahead, never behind!

*F*ATHER, I place my seconds, minutes, hours, and days in Your hands. I thank You for restoring my hope in the future.

Trust in him at all times; ye people,
pour out your heart before him:
God is a refuge for us.

PSALM 62:8

Hope and Humility

Though the LORD is supreme,
he takes care of those who are humble,
but he stays away from the proud.

PSALM 138:6 NCV

*M*any people believe that such things as money, possessions,

good looks, intelligence, and even power are the measure of their lives. None of these is inherently bad, yet none can predict happiness or instill a lasting sense of worth. What if we were to awaken one morning to find that our personal wealth and power had vanished? What if our attractiveness fails and our intelligence falters? Will hopelessness and despair overcome us?

God places little importance on outward appearances or the size of bank accounts. He measures our lives and hearts by a different standard. He teaches us that humility leads to greatness and that we achieve true success when we give ourselves to others. No measure other than the eternal love of God is a true measure.

*L*ORD, help me measure my life by Your standard so that my hope may shine brightly and never be disappointed.

God, examine me and know my heart;
test me and know my nervous thoughts.
See if there is any bad thing in me.
Lead me on the road to everlasting life.

PSALMS 139:23-24 NCV

Promises to Keep

My eyes stay open through the watches of the night,
that I may meditate on your promises.

PSALM 119:148 NIV

*W*hat would life be like without spring's warmth after a long and cold winter, rest after an exhausting and difficult day,

achievement after an intense and tiring struggle? Promises mark our lives. In fact, life is a promise in the process of being kept.

We may wonder at times if our life is no longer a bright promise. We lie awake in the night hours rehearsing our regrets that this may be so. But God is the great Promise Keeper. He is already aware of every poor choice, every lost opportunity, and every wasted second. He knows, and our mistakes grieve Him. He takes us as we are and restores hope to our lives.

*F*ATHER GOD, I will focus my eyes on Your faithfulness rather than on my own failures. I will look to You to help me fulfill the promise of all that my life can be.

*Y*our promise revives me;
it comforts me in all my troubles.

PSALM 119:50 NLT

*T*hy kingdom is an everlasting kingdom,
and thy dominion endureth throughout all generations.

PSALM 145:13

Someone to Count On

I have been young, and now am old;
yet have I not seen the righteous forsaken,
nor his seed begging bread.

PSALM 37:25

*L*ife is a long and complex journey that includes the tragic and the sublime, the good times and the bad times. Where can we turn when the bad times come? Who will keep our feet from stumbling when our eyes are filled with tears?

Even our closest friends and family can disappoint us—just as we can disappoint them. We can be confident that there is Someone who will never let us down, Someone who will be there for us in every season of our life, Someone who will lift our burdens and provide light for our feet as we walk along dark and lonely stretches of life's road. That Someone is God. He has promised never to leave us nor forsake us. He will walk with us every step of the way.

*L*ORD GOD, thank You for the comforting light of Your presence and the comforting strength of Your arm that lead me carefully through the dark places in my life.

The LORD keeps watch over you
as you come and go,
both now and forever.

PSALM 121:8 NLT

True Happiness

*Happy is he that hath the God of Jacob for his help,
whose hope is in the Lord his God.*

PSALM 146:5

Everyone pursues happiness, but few can define it. Is happiness the bright red apple dangling from the highest branch of the tree or the immense treasure buried somewhere underground? Is happiness the perfect person with whom to spend our life? Many times we lose hope of finding happiness simply because we're looking for it in the wrong places.

True happiness has less to do with outward circumstances than inward, and more to do with inward harmony than outward. True happiness is being anchored to our Creator, who knows us better than we know ourselves. True happiness isn't dependent on another person. It isn't dangling out of our reach or hiding deep underground. True happiness is found in the normal and mundane activities of our lives. We need only look inward and upward.

FATHER, as I lay my search at Your feet, restore my hope of finding true and lasting happiness.

Happy are those who respect the LORD
and obey him.
You will enjoy what you work for,
and you will be blessed with good things.

PSALMS 128:1-2 NCV

A New Song

*O*ur journey through life is not often easy, and each of us experiences times when we awaken to find ourselves battered and bruised, lost and forsaken, lying helpless along the side of life's road. Our resources gone and our strength spent, we wonder if there is hope for us. Will anyone come along to help?

God has promised that there is no circumstance from which He cannot rescue us. If we call out to Him, He will help us to our feet and provide comfort and support until our wounds heal and we are able to continue on our way. Though the circumstances that caused our fall may still be present, He has promised to walk with us, steadying our feet and imparting a new song of hope in our heart until we reach our final destination.

*L*ORD, I have no strength left. Lift me up, and give me new hope as I place my trust in You.

You will help me, Lord God,
and keep me from falling.

Psalm 54:4 cev

Woven in Secret

My frame was not hidden from you
when I was made in the secret place.
When I was woven together
in the depths of the earth,
your eyes saw my unformed body.

PSALM 139:15 NIV

A butterfly slips slowly from its cocoon and flutters away on a gentle breeze. Hidden from sight, it passed through a transforming

process known only to God, its Creator. In the same way that God made the butterfly, God fashioned each of us in secret—adding, subtracting, and shaping as only the great Creator can.

When we are tempted to question our inherent worth or to see ourselves as ugly and ungainly, we must remember that each of us is a treasured piece of God's own handiwork. We are an expression of the same creative force that placed the stars in the sky, strewed the flowers along the path, and raised up dry land in the midst of the sea. It is in the hand of the Artist that we have reason to hope.

*G*REAT CREATOR, when my failings cause me to lose a sense of my own value, I will hope in You, for You made me.

O come, let us worship and bow down:
let us kneel before the Lord our maker.

PSALM 95:6

*H*e brought me out into a broad place;
he delivered me, because he delighted in me.

PSALM 18:19 NRSV

Searching for Answers

*I look up to the mountains;
does my strength come from mountains?
No, my strength comes from GOD,
who made heaven, and earth, and mountains.*

PSALMS 121:1-2 THE MESSAGE

 *A*nswers to some questions are difficult to find. Why are we here? What purpose do our lives serve? Why is the life of a child cut short? Why is a strong and decent man cut down in his prime? Why must a young mother care for her children alone? Why do evil people prosper? Why do the ravages of war seem never to end?

We may never know the answers to these questions or the thousands of others drawn from the circumstances of our lives and from those around us. We can but place our hand in the hand of God and place our hope in His great wisdom and eternal love. We can rest in the knowledge that His intention for us is always good.

*F*ATHER, settle my heart, and help me to rest in the hope that one day all my questions will be answered as I stand in Your presence.

*N*ow I know that the L<small>ORD</small> saves his anointed;
he answers him from his holy heaven
with the saving power of his right hand.

P<small>SALM</small> 20:6 <small>NIV</small>

Safe and Sound

You will not fear the terror of the night,
or the arrow that flies by day,
or the pestilence that stalks in darkness,
or the destruction that wastes at noonday.

PSALMS 91:5-6 NRSV

*T*he eyes of the mother lion never leave her cubs as they scuffle playfully in the underbrush. Her instinct to guard and protect her little ones is intense and constant. She leaves them only long enough to secure food in the darkest hours of the night.

God watches over us more carefully than the most attentive lioness watches over her cubs. His eyes are always on us as we move through our days. Under His constant watchfulness, we find safety and wholeness. In the midst of danger and chaos, His presence is a source of hope and peace. When we call on Him for help, He comes quickly to rescue us and show us the way to safety.

*F*ATHER, I often feel fearful and insecure as I search for safety and protection for those I love and for me. From this day forward, I will place my trust in You and hope in Your faithfulness and love.

For he will hide me in his shelter in the day of trouble;
he will conceal me under the cover of his tent;
he will set me high on a rock.

PSALM 27:5 NRSV

An Enduring Peace

Great peace have they which love thy law:
and nothing shall offend them.

PSALM 119:165

*T*he starry grandeur of a midsummer night. The gentle gurgle of a languid river. The majestic stillness of a desert vista. The rolling

wave of unharvested grain. These are but a few of the natural expressions of peace and constancy God placed in the world.

In times of turmoil and distress, we can find moments of comfort and solace by gazing at the ageless beauty of a snowcapped mountain or by walking along a shell-strewn beach. For a while we enjoy the sense of peace. We hope that when we return to our everyday lives, the peace we found will remain with us. But only God can offer us lasting peace; only He can establish that lasting peace in our hearts.

*L*ORD GOD, bring peace and constancy to my heart, where pain and hopelessness now reside. I will hope in Your goodness.

You make the springs pour water into ravines,
so streams gush down from the mountains.
They provide water for all the animals,
and the wild donkeys quench their thirst.
The birds nest beside the streams
and sing among the branches of the trees.

PSALMS 104:10-12 NLT

A Steady Guide

Show me your ways, O LORD,
teach me your paths;
guide me in your truth and teach me,
for you are God my Savior,
and my hope is in you all day long.

PSALMS 25:4-5 NIV

*A*s we travel through unmarked trails and uncharted valleys of life, we sometimes become disoriented and lose our way. Feeling lost and alone, we're tempted to give up and abandon our dreams and ambitions.

When we lose our hope in the future, we grieve the heart of God. It is His desire to be our steady Guide, to take each of us by the hand and lead us through the tangled underbrush. He longs to walk with us each step of the way, pointing out the dangers and keeping our feet securely on the path. *I'll never leave you,* He tells us. *I'll illuminate your path with the light of My love.* No matter how lost and disoriented we become, our Guide is always available to help us find our way again.

*F*ATHER, as I travel through this life, I will take Your hand and trust You to lead me safely through each day.

*G*od is our protection and our strength.
He always helps in times of trouble.

PSALM 46:1 NCV

*H*e will not let your foot be moved;
he who keeps you will not slumber.

PSALM 121:3 NRSV

Second Chances

The LORD has mercy on those who respect him,
as a father has mercy on his children.

PSALM 103:13 NCV

*W*e all make mistakes, and sometimes the consequences of our mistakes are far-reaching, even irreversible. We feel we are doomed

to a life of frustration and despair, enslaved by the shadows of the past. In those difficult times, we can turn for help to the God of the rainbow, the God of second chances.

Even when our mistakes are so devastating that we cannot return to the lives we once knew, God's light can break through the threatening clouds and splash spectacular color across our lives. The consequences of our actions cannot be reversed, but God can add His miraculous touch and help us to build something new and uniquely beautiful. We only need to ask.

*L*ORD, You are the God of second chances. Grace my life with the miracle of Your touch, and help me begin again beneath the rainbow of Your faithful love.

I prayed to the Lord, and he answered me,
freeing me from all my fears.

PSALM 34:4 NLT

*H*e brought me up also out of an horrible pit,
out of the miry clay,
and set my feet upon a rock,
and established my goings.

PSALM 40:2

Seeking Success

Deal bountifully with your servant,
so that I may live and observe your word.

PSALM 119:17 NRSV

*S*uccess means different things to different people. To one it means wealth and fame; to another it means comfort and

contentment; to yet another it means accomplishment and fulfillment. We measure success by the degree to which we obtain the things that are most important to us.

But even when we achieve the goals we've set, we sometimes arrive at the finish line only to feel that our victory is empty and meaningless. Too late we realize that our furious run was in the wrong direction, and we experience feelings of sorrow and regret. God measures success in terms of faith, hope, and love. It is never too late to begin following His lead. Our consequent victory will be guaranteed to bring lasting satisfaction and a sense of true success.

*F*ATHER, help me to measure success by Your standard, trusting You to keep me headed in the right direction.

*L*ead me in the path of your commands,
because that makes me happy.
Make me want to keep your rules
instead of wishing for riches.
Keep me from looking at worthless things.
Let me live by your word.

PSALMS 119:35-37 NCV

Sharing God's Compassion

He, being *full of compassion,*
forgave their *iniquity, and destroyed* them *not:*
yea, many a time turned he his anger away,
and did not stir up all his wrath.

PSALM 78:38

Compassion does not exist in the natural world. A sudden wind uproots a tree with no regard for its usefulness. A boulder slips from its perch and crushes the flowers that flourish peacefully at its base. A stormy sea swallows a ship with no regard for the souls on board. Compassion is a characteristic that flows only from the heart of God.

The words and actions of others may hurt us. When we respond with a heart of compassion, however, we demonstrate that we are God's children. Our Heavenly Father has compassion on us even if we turn our back to Him, and He extends His hand to help us when we are lost and without hope. In the same way, we show our God-likeness by letting His compassion flow through us to others.

FATHER, thank You for pouring out Your compassion on me. And thank You for allowing me to share that compassion with others.

You, O Lord, are a compassionate and gracious God,
slow to anger, abounding in love and faithfulness.

Psalm 86:15 niv

Settled in Heaven

I will never stop loving him,
nor let my promise to him fail.
No, I will not break my covenant;
I will not take back a single word I said.

PSALMS 89:33-34 NLT

Each life has its share of disappointments—those dark moments when something we were counting on fails to materialize or

when someone we believe in lets us down. When we are struggling with the uncertainty that people and plans bring to our lives, it is a great comfort to know that God our Father will never fail us and that every plan He sets in place will prosper.

As we travel through the dark places on our journey through life, that old bandit *disappointment* may jump from the shadows and challenge us, threatening to rob us of our dreams. But disappointment cannot take what is ours as long as we remember that we are children of God. With God on our side, we need not fear the bandits that lurk in the shadows, for our future is secure and settled in Heaven!

UNFAILING FATHER, thank You for the one true thing in my life—Your faithful love. Help me to place my hope in You.

*T*he LORD looks at the world
from his throne in heaven, and he watches us all.

PSALM 33:13 CEV

*T*he counsel of the LORD standeth for ever,
the thoughts of his heart to all generations.

PSALM 33:11

Beginning Again

A tiny shoot thrusts itself through the crusty soil and pushes up into the sunlight. Fragile but determined, it presses on until one day it is covered with beautiful, exquisite flowers. Glorious, it stands in triumph—until the cold winter winds extinguish its beauty and strip it of all it has worked so hard to accomplish. But the story does not end. In season, spring breezes blow across the forsaken ground, and the sun once again warms the earth. Its hope restored, the little shoot, waiting beneath the soil, begins its journey again.

In many ways, our lives are as fragile as that tiny flower. At times, the cold winds of tragedy and loss blow over us, leaving us feeling withered and ruined. Just when we need Him most, God shines His light on our lives and warms our hearts so that we, too, can begin our journey again.

*F*ATHER GOD, help me push through the crusty soil of heartache and bloom again in the springtime of Your love.

*F*aithfulness will spring up from the ground,
and righteousness will look down from the sky.

PSALM 85:11 NRSV

*T*here is forgiveness with You,
That You may be feared.
I wait for the LORD, my soul waits,
And in His word I do hope.
My soul waits for the LORD.

PSALMS 130:4-6 NKJV

God's Fix for Fear

THE LORD is my light and my salvation; Whom shall I fear?
The LORD is the strength of my life;
Of whom shall I be afraid?

PSALM 27:1 NKJV

*F*ear is a predator. It crouches in the shadows and stalks its prey, waiting for any sign of weakness or vulnerability. When fear strikes, it can ravage our lives. It is a fierce and deadly enemy. Fear can rob us of family and relationships, destroy talent, and wipe out resources.

God has given us a mighty sword with which to fight the predator fear—our faith. Faith protects us from fear's torment and allows us to face each new day with hope and confidence. Faith frees us to tackle the real obstacles in our lives rather than to waste our energies dealing with difficulties that might never materialize. Our faith in God gives us the courage to face fear and drive it away.

*F*ATHER, thank You for the gift of faith that brings me hope and drives fear away.

O God, I praise your word.
I trust in God, so why should I be afraid?
What can mere mortals do to me?

PSALM 56:4 NLT

Facing the Sunlight

The LORD *God is a sun and shield:*
the LORD *will give grace and glory:*
no good thing *will he withhold*
from them that walk uprightly.

PSALM 84:11

*A*t times our lives are filled with the darkness of a polar night, with icy winds blowing across the frozen reaches of our hearts. We

wonder if the bone-chilling cold will ever release us from its deadly grip. In these times, we must place our hope in God, for He will not allow the icy darkness to reign forever in our lives. Eventually the sun will shine again, melting our ice-locked emotions and warming us inside and out.

The promise of renewed life comes with the sunlight of His love. We feel an unrestrained urge to turn our faces upward into its brilliance. The sunlight illuminates our hearts and chases away the long, cold night. We find that once again we are able to love and laugh and live; once again we are able to appreciate the good things God has placed in our lives. His mercy has wrought a bright, new morning!

*L*ORD GOD, thank You for bringing sunlight to my soul and warming my frozen heart.

To you, O Lord, I lift up my soul.

Psalm 25:1 nrsv

Light is sown for the righteous,
and gladness for the upright in heart.

Psalm 97:11

God's Majesty

Honor and majesty are before Him;
Strength and beauty are in His sanctuary.

PSALM 96:6 NKJV

God's majesty crowns the earth and the heavens. It is reflected in the splendor of the nighttime sky and the expanse of the ocean. It

is echoed in the strength of the mountains and the might of a river. It is evident in every loving gesture and simple act of forgiveness.

In times of loneliness and heartache, the visible signs of God's majesty bring us comfort, for they do more than decorate His greatness. They express His power, His constancy, and His resourcefulness—all available to us in our time of need. They remind us that our God is great and loving and kind, that our God is faithful and powerful enough to heal our broken hearts and to give us the will to go on.

GREAT GOD OF THE UNIVERSE, when I look around me and see Your majesty, I will rejoice in the fact that Your mighty hand is extended toward me. I will place my hope in You.

You formed the mountains by your power and armed yourself with mighty strength.

PSALM 65:6 NLT

Someone to Live For

Just tell me what to do and I will do it, LORD.
As long as I live I'll wholeheartedly obey.
Make me walk along the right paths
for I know how delightful they really are.

PSALMS 119:33-35 TLB

*T*ragedy and loss can leave us struggling with questions: Can any good come from our suffering? Can anyone take our confusion

and make sense of it all? Can anyone turn our life around and make it worth living?

When we ask if there is *something* to live for, God wants us to know that there is Some*one* to live for—Someone who can take our confusion and anger and create something beautiful, Someone who can wash away our loneliness and redeem our losses, Someone who can bring meaning to our lives simply by reminding us that we are created in His image.

*F*ATHER, thank You for the meaning and purpose You bring to my life. Thank You for allowing me to surrender my sorrow to You so that You can replace it with hope and happiness. You are truly *Someone* I can live for.

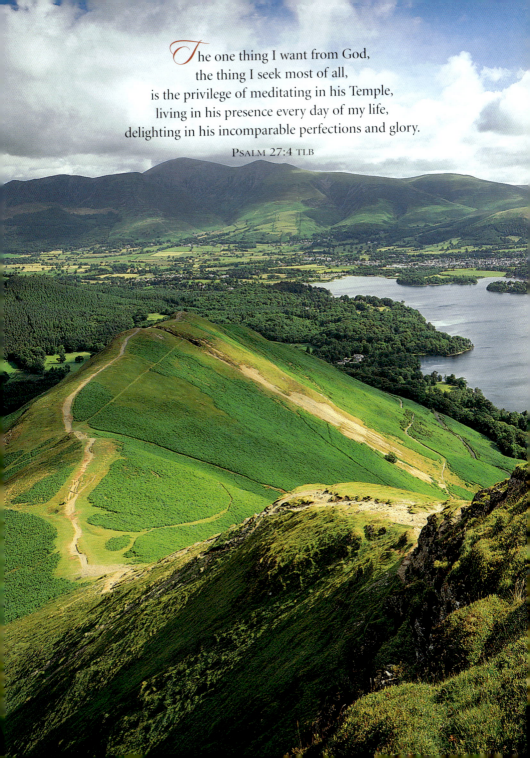

The one thing I want from God,
the thing I seek most of all,
is the privilege of meditating in his Temple,
living in his presence every day of my life,
delighting in his incomparable perfections and glory.

PSALM 27:4 TLB

Answered Prayers

Praise God,
who did not ignore my prayer
or hold back his love from me.

PSALM 66:20 NCV

Nothing can be louder or more intimidating than silence when we are waiting for an answer to our prayers. In the nighttime of the soul, God's silence thunders down at us, rattling our confidence and leaving us wondering if He has abandoned us.

At those times when God is silent, we must place our hope in two mighty truths: the truth of God's sovereignty and the truth of His faithfulness. God answers all our prayers, but always in His own time and in His own way. When we place our hope in Him, we will not be disappointed—even when the answer that comes is not what we expected.

When the heavens seem like brass, and we cannot hear His voice, we are wise to trust Him and wait patiently. It is in these times that our faith is tested, strengthened, and established.

FATHER GOD, when I do not hear Your voice, help me to rest in Your constant love as I wait for Your answer to my prayer.

Wait on the LORD;
Be of good courage,
And He shall strengthen your heart;
Wait, I say, on the LORD!

PSALM 27:14 NKJV

The LORD has heard my cry for help;
the LORD will answer my prayer.

PSALM 6:9 NCV

The Kite String

May He grant you according to your heart's desire,
And fulfill all your purpose.

A kite is a colorful spectacle as it sails high above the trees. Its reach seems unlimited, its flight unrestricted as it dips and weaves,

glides and bounces with the summer breeze. The kite may seem to be drifting free, but it is not. A taut string, almost invisible against the brightness of the day, keeps it from crashing to the ground or becoming entangled in the branches of a tree.

Our dreams are like the kite. They lift us above the trees and let us soar to new heights. Sometimes our dreams come crashing down because they are not safely anchored to God. When that happens, we must begin again, understanding that allowing God to hold the kite string is the very thing that will keep us aloft in a delightful pursuit of our heart's desires.

*L*ORD GOD, hold tight the string that anchors my heart to Yours, for my hope is ever in You.

I stay close to you;
you support me with your right hand.

PSALM 63:8 NCV

*O*ur heart shall rejoice in him,
because we have trusted in his holy name.
Let thy mercy, O LORD, be upon us,
according as we hope in thee.

PSALMS 33:21-22

God Shares Our Cares

The good man does not escape all troubles—
he has them too.
But the Lord helps him in each and every one.

PSALM 34:19 TLB

*A*ll of us face troubles and cares as we journey through life. At times, those cares can overwhelm us and leave us feeling desperate, alone, and hopeless. We must remember that our hope is in God. When we are struggling to keep our footing, He walks alongside, steadying our feet and helping us to carry our burdens.

Like a gentle shepherd, God guides us around the obstacles that block our path and through the waters that threaten to sweep us off our feet. Sometimes He carries our burdens, and sometimes He carries us. Through it all, we are never alone. He is always with us, sharing our cares, lightening our load, clearing the path before us, and assuring us that we will, one day soon, reach our destination.

*L*ORD GOD, thank You for sharing my cares and walking with me through all the troubles I encounter in this life. You are my Hope and my Helper.

You have made a wide path for my feet
to keep them from slipping.

PSALM 18:36 NLT

It is God who arms me with strength
and makes my way perfect.
He makes my feet like the feet of a deer;
he enables me to stand on the heights.

PSALMS 18:32-33 NIV

True North

*T*he strong and unmistakable light of the North Star has been beaming down from the heavens since the dawn of creation. The

North Star is a thing of beauty to the casual stargazer, but it holds much more significance for mariners, explorers, travelers, or those who have lost their way. For them, its radiant beam is a practical symbol of hope and safety, pointing the way to true north.

The light of God's love for us is strong and unmistakable. It also beams down on us from the heavens to fill us with hope and to guide us safely to our destination. When we have lost our bearings and don't know which way to turn, the light of God's love illuminates our way. As long as we follow its beam, His constant love will guide us safely home.

*F*ATHER, I will always keep my eyes on You and faithfully follow after Your love, for You alone are my True North.

$\mathcal{S}$end out your light and your truth;
let them guide me.
Let them lead me to your holy mountain,
to the place where you live.

PSALM 43:3 NLT

The Master Plan

Teach me how to live, O Lord.

PSALM 27:11 NLT

*A*n architect carefully creates a master plan for each new building, plotting all the details on paper before the first beam of wood is cut or the first nail is driven into place. The integrity of the

structure depends on the architect's skill and the degree to which the builders follow the master plan.

God has a master plan for each of our lives as well. When we disregard that plan or deviate from it in significant ways, we create an unstable structure that could come crashing down. When that happens, we must

cling to hope and turn to God, the Divine Architect. He is always ready to help us rebuild our lives. If it is too late for Master Plan A, then our faithful God will unfold the blueprint for Master Plan B.

*F*ATHER GOD, I will look to You as the Architect of my life. Help me build wisely, according to Your master plan.

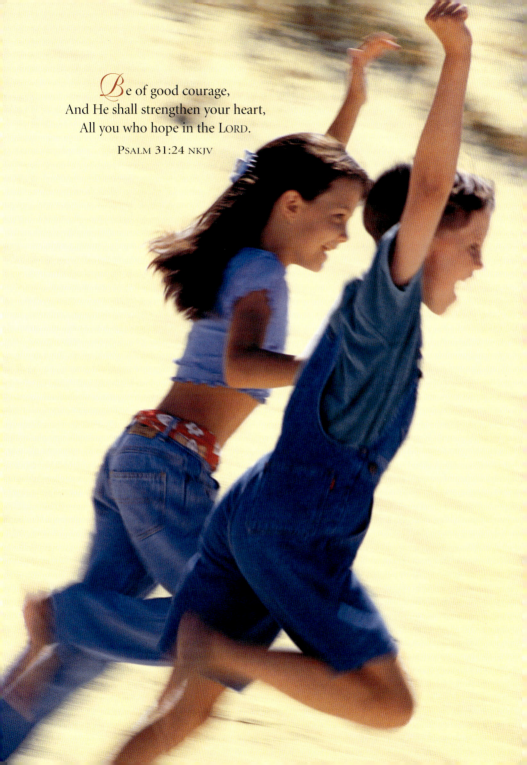

*B*e of good courage,
And He shall strengthen your heart,
All you who hope in the LORD.

PSALM 31:24 NKJV

A New Way of Thinking

Why art thou cast down, O my soul?
and why *art thou disquieted in me?*
hope thou in God:
for I shall yet praise him for *the help of his countenance.*

PSALM 42:5

Thoughts of failure, loss, and hopelessness can invade our minds, chasing, tormenting, and even destroying us. We run from

these thoughts, only to find that they are nipping at our heels. We try to hide, only to realize that they are stalking us.

When angry, bitter thoughts leave us running for our lives, God offers sanctuary and shelter. With one wave of His mighty hand, He chases away the brutal predators, and, one by one, He replaces them with thoughts of kindness, goodness, gentleness, and faith. Love transforms our minds, and hope restores our hearts. He promises that even though we may hear the wild beasts growling in the distance, they can never again harm us as long as we dwell in the shelter of His loving arms.

FATHER, I thank You for restoring hope to my heart and peace to my mind. You are my Savior and my God.

*T*hose who live in the shelter of the Most High
will find rest in the shadow of the Almighty.

PSALM 91:1 NET

*K*eep me as the apple of the eye,
hide me under the shadow of thy wings.

PSALM 17:8

Questions and Doubts

*Sustain me according to your promise, and I will live;
do not let my hopes be dashed.*

PSALM 119:116 NIV

In the utter stillness of a cavern deep underground, a single drop of water falls onto the surface of a small pond—and then

another and another and another. With time, the pond swells until the entire chamber is underwater. Doubt enters our lives in the same way—one drop at a time.

When we experience loss or disappointment, it is natural for us to have questions and experience doubt. But God wants us to bring our questions and doubts to Him. He wants to help us resolve our doubts and find the peace we so desperately need before we become imprisoned in a stony, doubt-filled chamber of our own making. The answers we seek may not come right away, but we can know God's true and lasting peace as we allow our doubts to flow out into the river of God's love.

FATHER, I bring my questions and doubts to You, and I trust that You will sustain me, for my hope is in You.

O LORD, HEAR me praying;
listen to my plea, O God my King,
for I will never pray to anyone but you.

PSALM 5:1 TLB

What Really Matters

They that sow in tears shall reap in joy.
He that goeth forth and weepeth,
bearing precious seed,
shall doubtless come again with rejoicing,
bringing his sheaves with him.

PSALMS 126:5-6

*A*thletes often find it necessary to look past the pain of injury and to continue playing in order to finish the game. They are trained

to focus their attention on what really matters—the win.

Loss and disappointment can cause us to lose sight of the things that are truly important in our

life. We want to leave the playing field and nurse our injury on the sideline; we want to give in to hopelessness and despair. When we let that happen, we forget that others are counting on us to stay in the game. We forget that God created us to win. The miraculous love of God can help us see past the pain and find a new level of strength and courage.

*F*ATHER, thank You for helping me stay in the game and focus on what really matters—winning in life!

God, I must keep my promises to you.
I will give you my offerings to thank you,
because you have saved me from death.
You have kept me from being defeated.
So I will walk with God
in light among the living.

PSALMS 56:12-13 NCV

Wonder and Awe

Trust the LORD *and his mighty power.*
Remember his miracles and all his wonders
and his fair decisions.

PSALMS 105:4-5 CEV

A newborn child lies sleeping in her mother's arms. She is a gift from God. How can we explain the softness of her skin, the

delicacy of her lashes, and the beautiful sculpture of her lips?

We cannot. Nor can we explain why God's gifts sometimes seem less than perfect—the little one whose life spans only one day, or the child who must face a lifetime with a disability. Asking why can leave us with overwhelming feelings of disappointment, even anger. But talking to God fills us with hope. He does not always give us the answers we seek, but He does gently remind us that every life—no matter how brief, no matter how challenged—is a miracle. Every life is worthy of our wonder and awe. God is always at our side, helping us to see the rainbow of promise through the veil of tears.

L ORD GOD, help me to see the miracles in my life through Your eyes.

The Lord is righteous in everything he does;
he is filled with kindness.
The Lord is close to all who call on him,
yes, to all who call on him sincerely.

Psalms 145:17-18 NLT

A Bright New Day

$\mathcal{P}$ast failures and disappointments can hover over us like leaden clouds, refusing to yield to the promise of sunlight and clear skies.

When we are surrounded by gray, it's difficult to dream of happier times. When we find ourselves in such a situation, God is always there to help.

When we call out to Him, He extends His hand to us and leads us out from under the foreboding clouds of the past and into the light of a new day. He offers hope for a new beginning. The journey into the sunlight is usually not an easy one, but God promises to walk with us every step of the way. A new life lies before us.

$\mathcal{F}$ATHER, I will place my hope in You as we walk together from beneath the dark clouds of the past and into the promise of the future.

*H*is anger lasts only a moment,
but his favor lasts a lifetime;
weeping may remain for a night,
but rejoicing comes in the morning.

PSALM 30:5 NIV

Simply Believe

I believe that I shall see the goodness of the LORD
in the land of the living.

PSALM 27:13 NRSV

*E*very fall as the cold winds of winter approach, flocks of birds
fly southward to warm climes and mild breezes. With no map to

guide them, they fly confidently,
accepting instinctively that their winter
refuges wait at the end of their
journey.

There are times in our lives when
we must fly south symbolically, away
from the winter winds of despair and
hopelessness. As we take flight, God promises that He will provide a
refuge for our troubled souls in His goodness, mercy, kindness, and
compassion. He asks us to believe that He will provide gentle breezes
for our journey. He asks us to believe that His never-failing love will
go with us wherever our journey takes us. *Simply believe,* He tells us
as we lean into the wind and surrender ourselves to healing and
hope.

*L*ORD GOD, my future is in Your hands.

I am the LORD your God,
who brought you up out of the land of Egypt.
Open your mouth wide and I will fill it.

PSALM 81:10 NRSV

*O*ur fathers trusted in You;
They trusted, and You delivered them.
They cried to You, and were delivered;
They trusted in You, and were not ashamed.

PSALMS 22:4-5 NKJV

Winning over Worry

Our LORD, we belong to you.
We tell you what worries us,
and you won't let us fall.

PSALM 55:22 CEV

*W*orry is really fear dressed in sheep's clothing. Disguised as a friend, it betrays us when we are most vulnerable, bringing before us images of what has been and images of what might be in its quest to steal our present and sabotage our future. Worry is a formidable threat to the tranquillity of our souls.

God says that we can win over worry by seeing it for what it is— a thief that can destroy our peace and steal our hope. When we turn to God and submit our anxious thoughts to Him, He promises to replace each one with pure and praiseworthy thoughts, thoughts that will help build our future rather than tear it down, thoughts that will restore our joy of living. Fear, stripped of its flimsy disguise, is then left to slink back into the shadows.

*F*ATHER, thank You for filling my mind with good thoughts so that I can win my battle with worry and fear.

THE LORD is my light and my salvation;
whom shall I fear?
the LORD is the strength of my life;
of whom shall I be afraid?

PSALMS 27:1-2

The Work of Waiting

Wait for the LORD;
Be strong, and let your heart take courage;
Yes, wait for the LORD.

PSALM 27:14 NASB

A strong and confident retriever strains against its leash, willing itself to be still. Every muscle twitches with expectation as it waits for its master's command. Like this magnificent animal, we often find waiting to be hard.

God knows that it is not easy for us to obey Him as we strain against our natural instincts; nevertheless, at times He asks us to wait. He also knows that when we wait on Him, we grow in faith and learn to respond with strength and wisdom rather than with haste and panic. Those times give us the opportunity to place our hope in God's faithfulness rather than to focus on our own need for gratification. When we face difficult times and find ourselves waiting for God to answer our prayers, we are preparing ourselves to receive His perfect answer.

*L*ORD GOD, when You ask me to wait, I will obey and place my hope in Your great love and faithfulness.

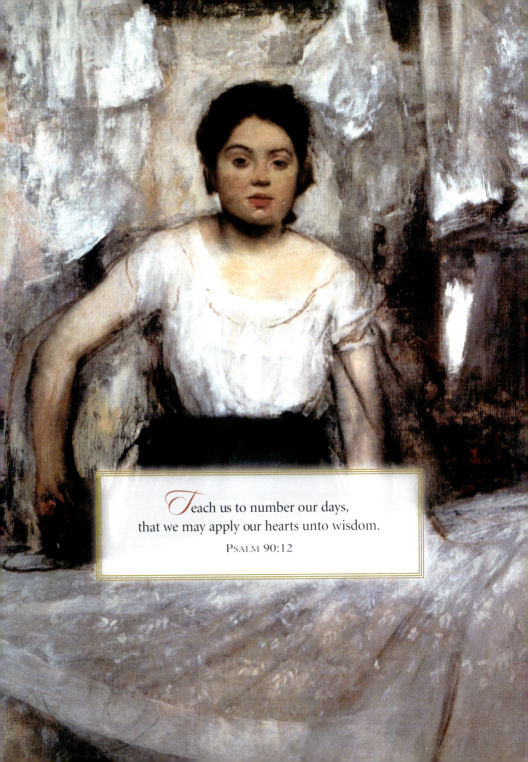

*T*each us to number our days,
that we may apply our hearts unto wisdom.

PSALM 90:12

Pausing for Power

You are awesome, O God, in your sanctuary;
the God of Israel gives power and strength to his people.

PSALM 68:35 NIV

*T*ragedy and loss can leave us feeling powerless, like a single flower that the wind whips and breaks. We may feel that we no

longer have control over the circumstances of our lives, and we may feel hopeless and alone. In the midst of those difficult times, we may feel that God is far away.

But God promises that He will always be with us. Even when anger and grief cause us to lose a sense of His presence, He is closer than the beating of our own hearts. He assures us that no tragedy can separate us from His amazing love. And He allows us to draw from His power to take responsibility for our lives again, to see past our heartache, and to find hope and healing in His presence.

*G*RACIOUS GOD, thank You for loving me, even in the midst of my anger and grief, and thank You for giving me the power and strength to live again.

I can lie down and go to sleep,
and I will wake up again,
because the L ORD gives me strength.

P SALM 3:5 NCV

Taking Hold of Grace

Grace is poured into thy lips:
therefore God hath blessed thee for ever.

PSALM 45:2

*G*od's grace is abundantly evident in the world around us. The rosy blush of the sunrise as it bursts above the horizon reminds us

that the long dark night is being replaced by the sparkling dawn of a brand-new day. The resplendent spectrum of the rainbow reminds us that the sun is busy chasing away the rain clouds. The whimsical laugh of a child at play reminds us that we, too, are children—God's children.

God's grace is evident in His creation, and it is God's gift to help us through the difficult times that life often brings our way. God's grace is the visible evidence of His everlasting love, and God offers His grace to us even when sorrow and grief threaten to drain the joy from our hearts.

*F*ATHER, when my heart is heavy with sorrow, Your grace lifts me up and gives me a new song to sing.

I will sing of your love and justice.
I will praise you, LORD, with songs.

PSALM 101:1 NLT

O sing to the LORD a new song,
for he has done marvelous things.
His right hand and his holy arm
have gotten him victory.

PSALM 98:1 NRSV

Returning to Life

You will show me the way of life,
granting me the joy of your presence
and the pleasures of living with you forever.

PSALM 16:11 NLT

*S*o far is the planet Pluto from the sun that it takes 248.5 years for Pluto to make its way around the outskirts of our solar system.

An observer on Pluto would view the sun as little more than a relatively bright star, with little ability to warm or illuminate the planet's icy consistency of frozen gas and metallic stone.

In our darkest hours of grief and loss, we may feel that our hearts have taken on the icy characteristics of a faraway planet. But no matter how we might *feel*, God promises that nothing—not one thing—can separate us from Him and His great love for us. When we place our hope in Him, we can count on His faithful tug to pull us back into a healing and life-sustaining orbit, where the brilliant rays of His presence will warm us, and the light of His endless love will illuminate all our dark places.

*F*ATHER, in the darkest hours of my life, I will place my hope in Your faithful love for me.

As high as the sky is above the earth, so great is his love for those who respect him.

Psalm 103:11 ncv

More than Enough

Many, O LORD my God, are thy wonderful works
which thou hast done,
and thy thoughts which are to us-ward:
they cannot be reckoned up in order unto thee:
if I would declare and speak of them,
they are more than can be numbered.

PSALM 40:5

A small boy stands in the sunshine, huffing and puffing in the direction of a dandelion his father is holding. When his boyish bluster finally reaches its target, the fluffy seeds abandon their stem

and float through the air to the music of the small boy's laughter. To the boy, this is a magical game, but to the flower, it is simple reproduction. Soon there are new dandelions popping up everywhere.

Troubles can multiply even more quickly than the sturdy, determined seeds of the dandelion flower. Whether we blow them into the air ourselves, or they simply fly on the wings of the wind, troubles can quickly overwhelm our lives. The good news is that God tells us that His thoughts are constantly on us, that He is devising ways to help us deal with each one. He is *always* more than enough to weed out the troubles in our lives!

*D*EAR FATHER, thank You for Your loving, watchful care over my life. I release my troubles to You, for I know that You are more than enough to handle them.

*Y*ou chart the path ahead of me
and tell me where to stop and rest.
Every moment you know where I am.

PSALM 139:3 NLT

Desert Streams

He turns a desert into pools of water,
a parched land into springs of water.

PSALM 107:35 NRSV

*O*n our journey, we sometimes pass through desert areas filled with nothing but uninviting cacti and sun-scorched sands as far as

the eye can see—seemingly barren wastelands on the landscape of our lives.

What we do not so quickly see is that the desert, as barren as it may appear, is teaming with robust life. Underground streams support a variety of hearty vegetation and lively creatures. God has not lessened the intensity of the sun's rays for their benefit. The sun shines on, but God has equipped the desert's flora and fauna to withstand the extremities of their home.

All of us pass through dry, parched areas in our journey through life. When we do, we must remember that God will faithfully provide for us, just as He has for the plants and creatures of the desert.

*L*ORD GOD, when I need streams in the deserts of my life, I will place my hope in Your faithfulness and love for me.

O GOD, thou art my God;
early will I seek thee: my soul thirsteth for thee,
my flesh longeth for thee in a dry and thirsty land,
where no water is.

PSALM 63:1

The Cost of Commitment

Commit everything you do to the Lord.
Trust him to help you do it and he will.

PSALM 37:5 TLB

*N*estled snugly among the branches of a gnarled blackjack oak, a bright red cardinal and its mate carefully guard a nest full of

eggs. Ever watchful, the adult birds vigorously defend the nest against predators. Until the eggs are hatched and the baby cardinals are mature enough to survive on their own, the adults are fully committed to their care.

God is even more committed to us than those amazing cardinals are to their little brood. When we are heartbroken and vulnerable, He is there to defend, sustain, and heal us in preparation for the day when we will fly high and strong on the currents of life. When we place our hope and trust in His faithfulness, we are never disappointed.

*F*ATHER GOD, when I feel weak and helpless, I will put my hope and trust in Your commitment to guard my life and nurse me back to health and wholeness.

*G*od, your love is so precious!
You protect people in the shadow of your wings.

PSALM 36:7 NCV

The Eyes of Understanding

Thy hands have made me and fashioned me:
give me understanding,
that I may learn thy commandments.

PSALM 119:73

The sunset is one of God's magnificent wonders. Sweeping across the horizon as if painted by God's own hand, it imbues the receding sunlight with indescribable splendor and signals that one day is giving way to another—a celestial changing of the guard.

Our lives are full of days as well, but we seldom pass as smoothly from one to the other. We fail to view the sunsets in our lives in the same way we do the sunrises. Endings can be just as beautiful as beginnings if we allow God to open the eyes of our understanding. When we truly realize the miracle of the sunset, we will no longer cling to the remains of the day. We will instead revel in its beauty, celebrating life to its fullest.

GREAT CREATOR, open the eyes of my understanding to appreciate the sunsets in my life.

*I*n ages past you laid the foundation of the earth,
and the heavens are the work of your hands.

PSALM 102:25 NLT

Divine Destiny

The LORD will work out his plans for my life—
for your faithful love, O LORD, endures forever.

PSALM 138:8 NLT

Whipped by the wind, the hungry flames of a wildfire devour everything in sight; the orange-red glow illuminates the night sky.

The morning light reveals the devastation in its aftermath. A sumptuous green forest has given way to rows of blackened stumps and a smoky expanse of charred ground.

God can renew even the blackened forest. In a few short months, new growth springs forth from the charred ground, and beautiful flowers and rich vegetation soon cover the ground like a warm, inviting blanket.

At times, we may feel that a raging wildfire has swept unchecked across our lives and left the rich colorful texture of our existence smudged and stunted. Even then we can rejoice, for God can also give new life to us. All He asks is that we place our hope in Him.

FATHER, thank You for Your promise of life and renewal.

Let the favor of the LORD our God be upon us,
and prosper for us the work of our hands—
O prosper the work of our hands!

PSALM 90:17 NRSV

A Wealth of Wisdom

The fear of the LORD is the beginning of wisdom;
all who follow his precepts have good understanding.
To him belongs eternal praise.

PSALM 111:10 NIV

*T*urbulence churns overhead as the distraught ocean whips against the ship. The captain struggles to find safe harbor. The

captain knows that under such trying circumstances it is easy to become disoriented and to be swept into treacherously shallow water where his vessel could be torn apart on the rocks. Rather than trust his own senses, the wise captain checks his compass and watches carefully for the beam from the lighthouse.

Similarly, we can become disoriented as we make our way through life's stormy seas. God promises that He will guide us with His wisdom and will light the troubled waters with the faithful beams of His love. When we place our hope in Him, we can be sure that we will find our way safely home.

*M*IGHTY GOD, thank You for the wisdom You provide as I navigate the stormy seas of my life. Thank You for the light of Your love that guides me safely into harbor.

The Lord on high is mightier than the noise of many waters,
yea, than the mighty waves of the sea.

Psalm 93:4

Take me out of the net that is hidden for me,
for you are my refuge.

Psalm 31:4 nrsv

Mysterious Ways

I do not concern myself with great matters
or things too wonderful for me.
But I have stilled and quieted my soul;
like a weaned child with its mother.

PSALMS 131:1-2 NIV

The sky darkens and ominous clouds form a wall from the ground upward as far as the eye can see. From its midst, a deafening roar and a swirling funnel emerge. Wind and

dust and debris fill the air as the tornado cuts a destructive swath across the landscape.

There are amazing exceptions. Amid the debris of one home, a solitary wall is still standing. On it hangs a knickknack shelf, which holds a fragile teapot, cup, and saucer—all mysteriously untouched by the storm's fury.

God tells us that even when devastating storms cut their terrible paths across our lives, the peace and love that He puts within us cannot be touched. He promises that He will never leave us, and He gives us the strength and the courage to rebuild our lives and look with hope into a bright future.

HEAVENLY FATHER, Your mysterious ways give me love, peace, and hope in the midst of life's most powerful storms.

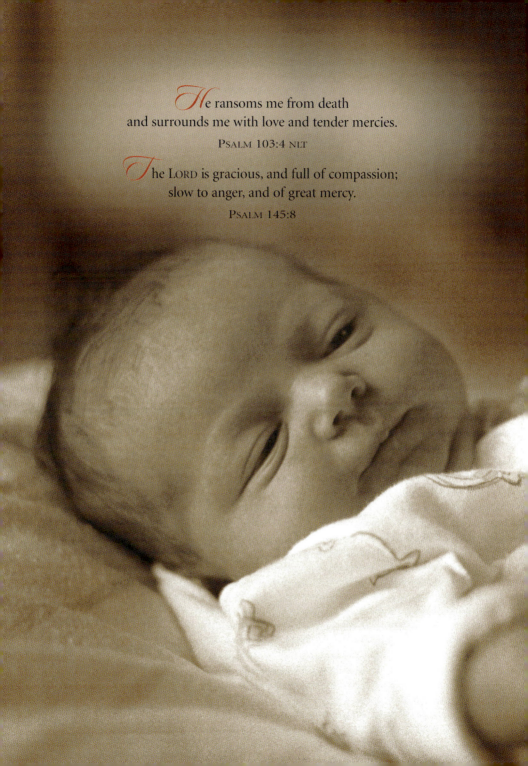

*H*e ransoms me from death
and surrounds me with love and tender mercies.

PSALM 103:4 NLT

*T*he LORD is gracious, and full of compassion;
slow to anger, and of great mercy.

PSALM 145:8

Facing the Future

When anxiety was great within me,
your consolation brought joy to my soul.

PSALM 94:19 NIV

A giant tortoise lumbers contentedly along on its way to nowhere, stopping often to nibble on the grass. A loud noise pierces

the air, and a shadow crosses the tortoise's path. The tortoise stops right where it is, pulls its head into its shell, and shuts out the world.

All of us experience times when we are tempted to pull into ourselves to avoid emotional pain, fear, or disappointment. Brief periods of solitude can often help us process our thoughts and gain inner strength. However, just as the tortoise would soon starve if it remained in its shell indefinitely, so, too, would we starve emotionally if we remained walled up inside ourselves. God promises to help us face our circumstances and walk forward with confidence and hope.

*G*RACIOUS FATHER, thank You for drawing me out of my fearful, anxious shell and into the light of Your love. Thank You for new promise and purpose for my life.

*T*he LORD is close to the brokenhearted,
and he saves those whose spirits have been crushed.

PSALM 34:18 NCV

*C*reate in me a clean heart, O God;
and renew a right spirit within me.

PSALM 51:10

Rising to the Challenge

Be of good courage,
And He shall strengthen your heart,
All you who hope in the Lord.

PSALM 31:24 NKJV

stony peak rises in the distance—cold and formidable against the early morning sky. To the casual observer, it would seem to be an unforgiving fortress, off limits to man or beast. Then a climber is spotted scaling the face of the peak, inching upward—one toehold, one handhold at a time.

When we look ahead and see nothing but cold, stony, uninviting peaks crowding the landscape of our lives, we must not lose heart. God has promised to help us tackle each and every challenge. He brings us hope and encouragement; He urges us upward one toehold and one handhold at a time. He holds us steady as we make our way to the summit. He restores our hope as we gaze down into the lush valley on the other side.

LORD GOD, when my future seems to be filled with stony peaks, I will place my hope in Your strength and faithfulness.

*Y*es, he alone is my Rock,
my rescuer, defense and fortress.
Why then should I be tense with fear
when troubles come?

PSALM 62:2 TLB

Songs for the Soul

Through each night I sing his songs,
praying to God who gives life.

PSALM 42:8 NLT

Atop the fence post, a robin lifts its head toward heaven and its voice in song. Other troubadours take up the chorus, and a jubilee  of birdsong fills the air, refreshing the heart of their Creator. Why does the robin sing? It sings because it must; it was designed to bring constant praise to God.

Like the robin, we are God's creation. Unlike the robin, however, we have been given a greater gift. We have been given a will. When we lift our voices to God, it is because we *choose* to do so. Our songs of praise delight the heart of God. He knows that our songs bring comfort, solace, and refreshment to our own lives, strengthening us in difficult times.

FAITHFUL CREATOR, teach me to sing Your praises during good times and bad times. Strengthen, comfort, and heal me as I lift my voice in song.

Clap your hands, all you peoples;
shout to God with loud songs of joy.
For the LORD, the Most High, is awesome,
a great king over all the earth.

PSALMS 47:1-2 NRSV

Ice Storms

Icicles hang from the eaves of houses and the branches of trees. They are visible testaments that cold winds and freezing

temperatures followed the rain too closely. The rays of the sun beat down upon them to melt them away drop by drop.

The bitter winds of calamity blow across our lives; sometimes they follow too soon on the heels of other losses and disappointments. Our tears turn to ice. We are weighed down, and our emotions are locked in an icy grip.

Even then, God is able to reach us with the sunlight of His love, melting away our frozen places. As long as we place our hope in Him, no icy prison can hold us.

L{ORD} G{OD}, when my heart seems to be locked in sorrow's icy grip, I will look to You for help and place my hope in the sunlight of Your love.

Whoever is wise, let him heed these things
and consider the great love of the LORD.

PSALM 107:43 NIV

I am constantly aware of your unfailing love,
and I have lived according to your truth.

PSALM 26:3 NLT

Leaping for Joy

*N*ot far offshore, a pod of whales moves smoothly through
the water on the way to warmer seas. As the whales pass, the

magnificent creatures take turns breaching,
thrusting their enormous bodies high into
the air before splashing on their bellies or
their backs.

Those who study whales now believe
they breach for only one reason—they want
to! Perhaps they enjoy the way the sun feels on their skin; perhaps
they enjoy the rush of air. Whatever the case, it appears that whales
leap from the water for the sheer joy it brings them.

No matter what our circumstances might be, we, too, are able to
leap for joy, reminding ourselves that God has given us many
blessings—the unfailing miracles of His love, His peace, and His
promise that He will always be with us, comforting, encouraging,
and leading.

*L*OVING GOD, thank You for the blessings You have placed in my
life—blessings so wonderful that they cause me to leap for joy.

I will go to the altar of God,
to God who is my joy and happiness.
I will praise you with a harp,
God, my God.

PSALM 43:4 NCV

Autumn Leaves

*Show me, O LORD, my life's end
and the number of my days;
let me know how fleeting is my life.*

PSALM 39:4 NIV

*T*he leaves of autumn—burnished gold, dusty red, muted orange, and bright yellow—float through the air and cover the ground, a glorious tribute to what was and soon will be no more. Does it seem strange that God would invest such exquisite beauty in a season of dying? He knows that unless we are willing to celebrate the end of what we know, we will not enter into what is yet to be.

It doesn't matter what we are facing, whether the end of our physical lives, the end of a lifelong dream, the end of a marriage or a long-term relationship, the passing of our youth, or our children leaving home. God encourages us to see the beauty in the leaves of autumn and trust Him for what lies ahead, including the glory of Heaven. God will never disappoint us when we place our hope in Him.

*A*LL-KNOWING FATHER, help me to appreciate the beauty of autumn leaves as I walk with You into the future.

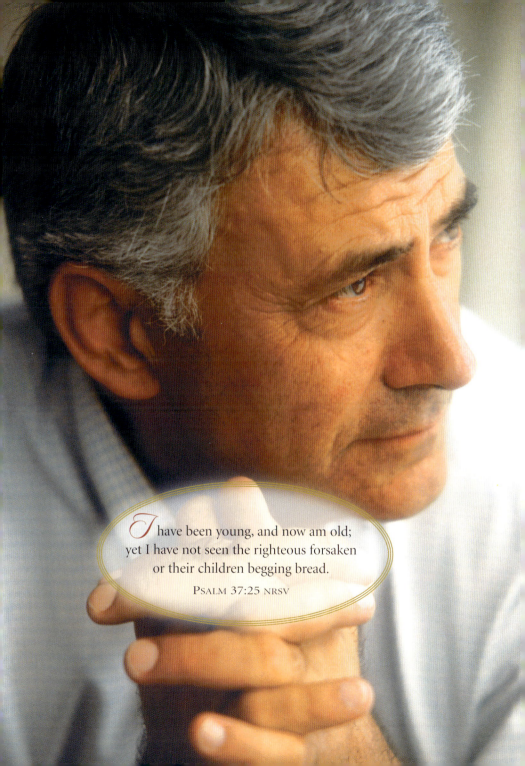

$\mathcal{I}$ have been young, and now am old;
yet I have not seen the righteous forsaken
or their children begging bread.

PSALM 37:25 NRSV

Staying Steady Through Tough Times

As for me, I will always have hope;
I will praise you more and more.

PSALM 71:14 NIV

The tendrils of ivy climb the sides of the brick structure until they cover every square inch. Ivy stems are strong, hearty, and almost

unbreakable, and they grip the surface so tightly that only the most determined effort can dislodge them. Ivy is capable of weathering the extremes of both heat and cold without withering and falling away.

When we place our hope in God, we are clinging to Him in the same tenacious way that ivy clings to brick and mortar. When the sun is warm and the rain is gentle, we grow strong and hearty, reaching and moving as we strengthen our grip on God's never-failing love. Then when the strong winds blow and the rain beats at us, when the sun scorches our leaves and we feel dry and parched to the root, we know that we can hang on. We cannot be moved.

MIGHTY GOD, help me to cling to You like ivy clings to the brick.

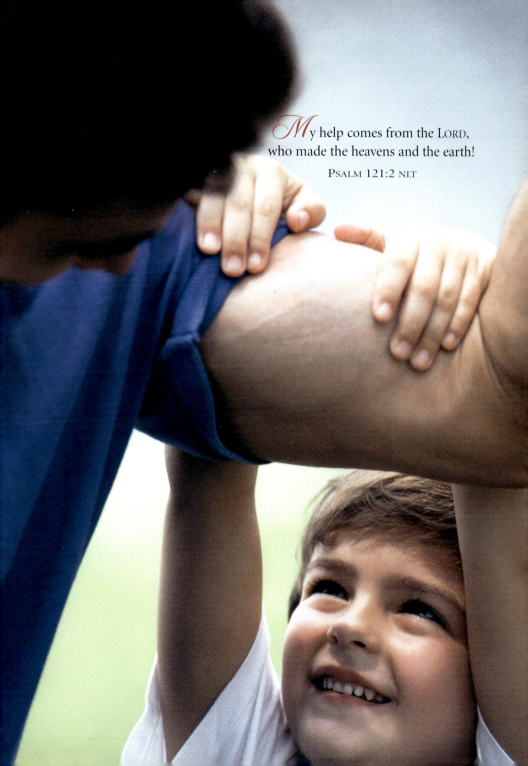

*M*y help comes from the LORD,
who made the heavens and the earth!

PSALM 121:2 NLT

God Is on the Throne

The LORD is in His holy temple;
the LORD's throne is in heaven;
His eyes behold, His eyelids test the sons of men.

PSALM 11:4 NASB

A tiny child lies in her crib, smiling broadly as her mother coos from just above the railing. The moment her mother steps out of sight, the child's sweet smile disappears. She begins to whimper.

Because she can no longer see her mother or sense her presence, the child believes she has been abandoned.

As we begin to put our hope in God, we are in many respects like small children. We cannot grasp His greatness or the eternal aspects of His character. When we experience difficult times and do not immediately sense His presence, we may feel that He has left us and no longer cares about us. As we grow in our faith, we realize that there is more to God than what we can see and understand. His eyes of love never leave us. His hand is always there to pick us up and hold us tenderly.

*F*ATHER GOD, help me as I grow in hope and faith.

*A*s for me, my prayer is to you, O LORD.
At an acceptable time, O God,
in the abundance of your steadfast love, answer me.

PSALM 69:13 NRSV

*S*o, LORD, what hope do I have?
You are my hope.

PSALM 39:7 NCV

A Pattern of Patience

I waited patiently for the LORD;
he inclined to me and heard my cry.

PSALM 40:1 NRSV

*T*ulips and daffodils, in all the brilliant colors of spring, hide throughout the long winter in tight little shells deep beneath the

surface of the soil. We barely know they exist as the wind blows and the cold holds us in its grip.

But with the first warming breeze of spring, we notice green shoots bursting through the surface of the soil. Soon waving everywhere are the red, pink, and yellow flags that represent God's faithful promise that summer and winter, springtime and harvest will continue on the earth, and in our lives, each at its appointed time.

We must be patient and cling to our hope in God. In His perfect time, the ambassadors of spring will burst forth in our lives once more.

*L*ORD GOD, thank You for the promise of springtime in my life. I will wait patiently through the difficult seasons and hope earnestly in Your faithfulness.

*Y*ou will increase my honor
and comfort me once again.

PSALM 71:21 NIV

*Y*ou made me suffer a lot,
but you will bring me back from this deep pit
and give me new life.
You will make me truly great and take my sorrow away.

PSALMS 71:20-21 CEV

Wings of Mercy

O taste and see that the LORD is good:
blessed is the man that trusteth in him.

PSALM 34:8

*H*igh above the treetops, a black-winged hawk soars
majestically. The bird's swoops and glides appear effortless as it

moves along on the late afternoon
breezes. It seems to fear nothing
above or below as it sails back and
forth, up and down, soaking up
the last, lingering rays of the sun.

In the midst of difficult times, it's tempting to look up at the
hawk and wish that we, too, could sail along on gentle breezes, high
above our painful circumstances. During those seasons when our
strength seems almost gone, God wants us to know that He is there
to sweep us up onto His mighty wings of mercy and grace. There we
find rest, comfort, and healing for our broken hearts and wounded
spirits.

*F*ATHER, when my life seems unbearably painful, I will place my
hope in You. I will forsake my own failing strength and rest on Your
wings of mercy.

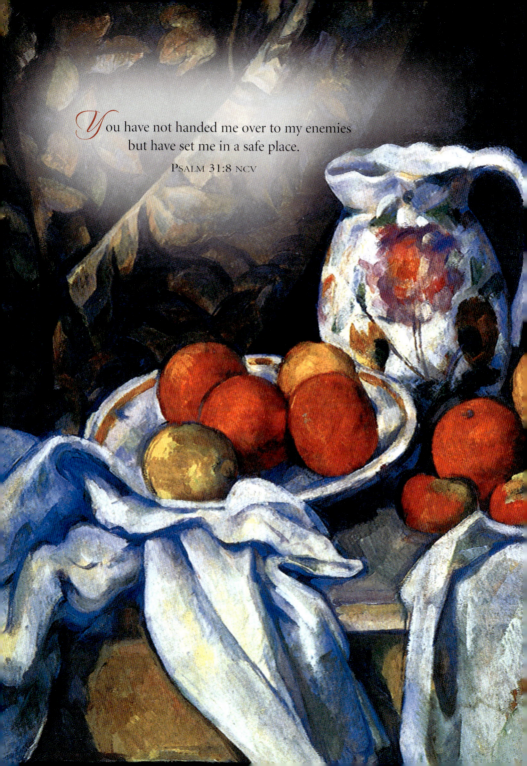

*Y*ou have not handed me over to my enemies
but have set me in a safe place.

PSALM 31:8 NCV

Sure Footing

Let everyone bless God and sing his praises,
for he holds our lives in his hands.
And he holds our feet to the path.

PSALMS 66:8-9 TLB

 o steep and treacherous are the paths along the walls of the
Grand Canyon that those who wish to traverse them rarely set out on

foot. They depend on remarkable animals
with hoofs designed to hug the narrow, dusty
paths and bodies proportioned for maximum
strength, endurance, and balance.

In the course of our lives, many of us will
encounter certain mountain paths that are
simply too difficult and dangerous for us to

attempt alone. When we set out on those trails, God promises that
we can depend upon Him to keep us from falling. He will provide
the assistance we need to secure our footing and to carry our burdens
safely to the top of the canyon wall.

 AITHFUL GOD, when I must follow a steep and treacherous path on
my journey through life, I will place my hope and trust in Your
promise to help me reach my destination safely.

*H*e will command his angels concerning you
to guard you in all your ways;
they will lift you up in their hands,
so that you will not strike your foot against a stone.

PSALMS 91:11-12 NIV

The Source of Hope

Now, LORD, *what wait I for? my hope* is *in thee.*

PSALM 39:7

The song of the robin, the majesty of snow-covered mountain peaks, the lustrous beauty of a spring flower, and the predictable movement of the stars in the night sky are but a few of the wonders

that point us to God, the Source of all hope.

They are reminders that no circumstance—poverty, pain, sickness, loss, disappointment, grief, even the prospect of our own death—can steal our hope when it is safely anchored in God.

FATHER OF ALL HOPE, thank You for promising never to leave my
side as I walk through the dark, confusing, lonely,
and painful places in my life.

Thank You for Your promise to replace my clouds of despair with
the brilliant, penetrating light of Your everlasting love. Thank You
for filling my heart with peace and my mind
with wisdom and understanding.

Thank You for a voice with which to sing
Your praises with my whole heart. Amen.

Shout with joy to the LORD, O earth!
Worship the LORD with gladness.
Come before him, singing with joy.

PSALMS 100:1-2 NLT

Enter his gates with thanksgiving;
go into his courts with praise.
Give thanks to him and bless his name.
For the LORD is good.
His unfailing love continues forever,
and his faithfulness continues to each generation.

PSALMS 100:4-5 NLT

If you have enjoyed this book, you will also enjoy other gift books available from your local bookstore.

GIFTS FROM MY GARDEN

GIFTS FROM MY FRONT PORCH

DAILY BLESSINGS FOR MY HUSBAND

DAILY BLESSINGS FOR MY WIFE

DAILY BLESSINGS FOR MY SECRET PAL

LETTERS FROM GOD

LETTERS FROM GOD FOR TEENS

LIGHTHOUSE PSALMS

FRIENDSHIP PSALMS

LOVE PSALMS

PSALMS FOR FATHERS

PSALMS FOR MOTHERS

PSALMS FOR WOMEN

PSALMS FOR THE HEART

If this book has impacted your life, we would like to hear from you.

Please contact us at:

Honor Books
Department E
P.O. Box 55388
Tulsa, Oklahoma 74155

Or by e-mail at:
info@honorbooks.com